"My Teenage Son's Goal in Life Is to Make Me Feel 3,500 Years Old"

*and Other
Thoughts on Parenting
from*

Dave Barry

"My Teenage Son's Goal in Life Is to Make Me Feel 3,500 Years Old"

*and Other
Thoughts on Parenting
from*
Dave Barry

**Andrews McMeel
Publishing**

Kansas City

ISBN: 0-7407-1526-7

Library of Congress Catalog Card Number: 00-108466

Book design by Lisa Martin
Illustrations by Matthew Taylor

Parenthood is not unlike the Space Mountain ride at Disney World, in the sense that both experiences involve zooming along in a carefree manner, then suddenly having your stomach get collapsed like a stomped-on Dixie cup by violent unexpected high-speed turns.

Times have changed. I found this out the night of my son's first dance party, when, fifteen minutes before it was time to leave for the party, he strode impatiently up to me, wearing new duds, looking perfect in the hair department, and smelling vaguely of—Can it be? Yes, it's *Right Guard*—and told me that we had to go *immediately* or we'd be late. This from a person who has never, ever shown the slightest interest in being on time for anything, a person who was three weeks late to his own *birth*.

When we get to the tax form question about how much, exactly, we spent on "child care," we are going to have some questions of our own, including: What about Captain Skyhawk? Captain Skyhawk is a Nintendo game that I purchased for my son for Christmas because I am a bad parent who wishes to rot his mind. It cost $41.99, and I definitely view that as a child-care expense.

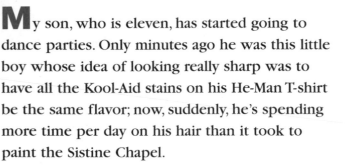

My son, who is eleven, has started going to dance parties. Only minutes ago he was this little boy whose idea of looking really sharp was to have all the Kool-Aid stains on his He-Man T-shirt be the same flavor; now, suddenly, he's spending more time per day on his hair than it took to paint the Sistine Chapel.

I know how we can solve our national crisis in educational funding: Whenever the schools needed money, they could send a letter to all the parents, saying, "Give us a contribution right now, or we're going to hold a Science Fair." They'd raise billions.

Your Prom magazine (published by *Modern Bride*) is chock-full of prom advice and glossy color promwear advertisements featuring models who look exactly like what high school students would look like if they were all professional models and resembled Tom Cruise or Julia Roberts and didn't have acne.

My son is going to parties where the boys dance with actual girls. This was unheard of when I was eleven, during the Eisenhower administration. Oh, sure, our parents sent us to ballroom-dancing class, but it would have been equally cost-effective for them to simply set fire to their money.

The computer is a great teaching tool for young people. For example, my home computer has an educational program that enables you to control an entire simulated planet—its ecology, its technology, its weather, etc. My ten-year-old son and his friends use this program a lot, and we've all learned some important ecological lessons, the main one being never, ever put ten-year-old boys in charge of a planet ("Let's see what happens when you have volcanoes *and* nuclear war!").

I was a counselor at a place called Camp Sharparoon. My group, consisting of nine-year-old boys, went by the Indian name "Schaghticokes" (pronounced SCAT-a-cooks), which I believe is the Indian word for "boys who are too scared to go out to the latrine in the woods at night." On camping trips our primary wilderness pioneer activity was hanging blankets out to dry, the result being that there was no wildlife for two hundred miles downwind of our campsite.

My high school had a strict dress code, administered by Mr. Sabella, who enforced it by picking offenders up by their necks and shaking them like deceased chickens. Schools today have much looser dress codes, something like "Students must wear clothes, unless they have an excuse." You see every dress style: Surfer, Preppy, Hippie, Intellectual, Bimbette, Cheerleader, Jockstrap, Punk, and Young Felon of Tomorrow, to name just a few. Sitting in the Palmetto High School office, I'm admiring the haircut of a young man who is virtually bald on the left side of his head and has shoulder-length hair on the right. I'm wondering what administrative technique Mr. Sabella would have used on this young man. Probably firearms.

My son's new sneakers cost approximately as much as an assault helicopter but are more technologically advanced. They are the heavily advertised sneakers that have little air pumps inside. This feature provides an important orthopedic benefit: It allows the manufacturer to jack the price up. Also it turns the act of walking around into a highly complex process. "Wait!" my son will say, as we're rushing off to school, late as usual. "I have to pump more air into my sneakers!" Because God forbid you should go to school underinflated.

Waves of students are surging in and out of the high school's main office, trying to find out which rooms they're supposed to go to. This is determined by a complex schedule apparently designed so that, whenever the bell rings, every student in the school has to bump into every other student to get to the next class.

The Halloween of 1978, the community where I lived decided to hold a party where the neighborhood children would have some traditional Halloween fun such as bobbing for apples, the theory being that they'd do less traditional Halloween property damage if their lungs were full of water.

I have done a detailed scientific survey of several other parents, and my current estimate is that sneakers now absorb 83 percent of the average U.S. family income. This has to stop. We need Congress to pass a law requiring the sneaker industry to return to the system we had when I was growing up, under which there was only one kind of sneakers, namely U.S. Keds, which were made from Army surplus tents and which cost about $10, or roughly $1 per pound.

Babies want to put everything in the entire world except food into their mouths. As far as babies are concerned, the sole function of the world is to provide objects for them to drool on.

● ● ●

If you let your baby continue to stick things into his or her mouth, he or she will have a hard time later in life. I mean, suppose your child goes to a major Wall Street law firm for a job interview, and ends up putting all the waiting-room magazines and ashtrays in his or her mouth. He or she would make a poor impression, and would end up having to be a bum or work for the government.

These days they're not allowed to show violence on television except on Saturday-morning cartoon shows for children aged five and under. The rest of us are stuck with TV talk shows in which people drone on endlessly about sex but never actually do anything on the screen. After watching these shows for a few hours, viewers tend to get bored and go out on the street and commit acts of violence.

Many of you young persons out there are seriously thinking about going to college. (That is, of course, a lie. The only things you young persons think seriously about are loud music and sex. Trust me: These are closely related to college.)

• • •

I am waging a battle with my son to keep him normal, defined as "like me, but with less nose hair."

One reason why I'm qualified as a health-care expert is that I have a son whose life's goal is to obtain at least one suture in every emergency room in North America. This means I spend a lot of time filling out medical forms and reading correspondence from the insurance company. You know how scientists have spent years beaming powerful radio signals into space, trying to contact alien life forms? Well, they could save themselves a lot of trouble by simply visiting my insurance company, because the correspondence I receive clearly is not being generated by earthlings.

Dave Barry's Baby Game: Oklahoma Baby Chicken Hat

Grasp your baby firmly and put it on your head like a hat, stomach down. Then stride around the room and cluck like a chicken to the tune of "Surrey with the Fringe on Top," bouncing in time to the music. *(Note: Wear protective clothing.)*

This game will teach your baby many meaningful lessons, the main one being that the world is full of deranged people.

I am being rapidly aged by Rob's choice of radio stations. The one he now prefers is operated by one of the most dangerous and irresponsible forces on earth: college students.

My son got his ear pierced. He's twelve. For twelve years I worked hard to prevent him from developing unnatural bodily holes, then he went out and got one on purpose. At a *shopping mall.* It turns out that minors can have their earlobes assaulted with sharp implements by shopping-mall-booth personnel who, for all we know, have received no more formal medical training than is given to burrito folders at Taco Bell.

20

Summer's almost here, and it's time for you parents to decide about summer camp. First you need to select the type of camp. Today, in addition to the traditional category of Camps with Comical Names Like "Camp Wabonga," there are many specialty camps, including Tennis Camp, Art Camp, Drama Camp, Diet Camp, Gorge Yourself Camp, Homesickness Camp, Cramp Camp, Enemy Camp, and Space Camp, at the end of which your child is actually launched into orbit (this one is all booked up).

Most people make babies out to be very complicated, but the truth is they have only three moods:

Mood One: Just about to cry.

Mood Two: Crying.

Mood Three: Just finished crying.

Niagara Falls is a geological formation caused by the Great Lakes being attracted toward gravity. Also limestone is involved. We learned these facts from a giant-screen movie about the Falls that we paid to get into after the children became bored with looking at the actual Falls, a process that took them perhaps four minutes. They are modern children. They have Nintendo. They have seen what appears to be a real dinosaur eat what appears to be a real lawyer in the movie *Jurassic Park*. They are not about to be impressed by mere water.

The most important thing to remember about raising your baby is that you must not take anyone's advice, except, of course, mine. Many people, such as your parents, will try to advise you, but you must ignore them. If they knew so much about raising kids, they wouldn't have screwed you up so badly.

You can get almost anything you want from
your parents, provided you're not afraid to whine.
I remember when I was twelve and really *needed*
a BB gun. My parents didn't want me to have one,
on the grounds that I might shoot my brother.
But I put together a string of about thirty-five days
during which I was without question the most
sniveling, obnoxious child in the entire world.
It got to the point where, to preserve their
sanity, my parents had to either give me
a BB gun or hire someone to kidnap me.
They eventually elected to buy me a
BB gun, mainly because it was cheaper.
I was so grateful that I didn't shoot my
brother for three or four days.

This is the time of year to gather up your family and all your available money and decide what you're going to do on your summer vacation. You should get an opinion from everybody, including your children, because, after all, they are family members, too, even though all they do is sit around and watch television and run up huge orthodontist bills and sneer at plain old affordable U.S. Keds sneakers, demanding instead elaborate designer athletic footwear that costs as much per pair as you paid for your first car. On second thought, the heck with what your children want to do. You can notify them of your vacation plans via memorandum.

I am constantly seeing young people with the bills of their baseball caps pointing *backward.* This makes no sense, young people! If you examine your cap closely, you will note that it has a piece sticking out the front, called a "bill." The purpose of the bill is to keep sun off your face, which, unless your parents did a great many drugs in the '60s (ask them about it!), is located on the *front* of your head. Wearing your cap backward is like wearing sunglasses on the back of our head, or wearing a hearing aid in your nose. (Perhaps you young people are doing this also. Uncle Dave doesn't want to know.)

If you're looking for a family vacation that involves watching enormous quantities of water go off a cliff, you can't beat Niagara Falls. We went there recently with several other families, and our feeling of awe and wonderment can best be summed up by the words of my friend Libby Burger, who, when we first beheld the heart-stopping spectacle of millions of gallons of water per second hurtling over the precipice and thundering into the mist-enshrouded gorge below, said, "I have to tinkle."

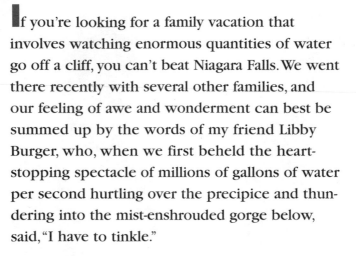

College students are in on the plot with my son to make me feel old. Not long ago I was sitting on a beach near a group of male college students who were talking about a bungee-jumping excursion they had taken. They were bragging about the fact that they had leaped off the tower in the *only* cool way, which is head-first and backward. They spoke with great contempt about a group of fathers—that's the term they used, "fathers," making it sound as though it means "people even older than Phoenicians"—who had jumped off feet-first, which the college students considered to be pathetic. This made me feel *extremely* old, because I personally would not bungee-jump off the *Oxford English Dictionary.*

Summer camps make a determined effort to hire staff members who meet the highest possible standards of maturity and responsibility. But eventually they give up and hire college students.

• • •

The greatest threat to your baby is educational toys, which you are required by federal law to buy several dozen of. Educational toys are advertised in baby magazines, which arrive by the thousands in the mail when you have a baby. In a typical ad, a baby is looking thoughtfully (for a baby) at two pieces of plastic. According to the ad, the pieces of plastic are helping the baby "acquire skills of problem solving." In fact, the only problem the baby is solving is the problem of how to get both pieces in his mouth.

Let me assure you that I want to play a responsible role in my wife's pregnancy. I am willing to pace for *hours* in the waiting room with the other fathers-to-be and old copies of *National Geographic.* I am willing to go to classes on how to pace in the waiting room. But at our classes we don't talk about pacing: We talk about *what goes on inside a pregnant person's body.* I don't want to *know* what goes on inside my *own* body. I think if the Good Lord had wanted us to know what goes on inside our bodies, He would have given us little windows.

If you were to open up a baby—and I am not for a minute suggesting that you should—you would find that 85 to 90 percent of the space reserved for bodily organs is taken up by huge, highly active drool glands.

We're going to have to do something about children's television. Today's children watch shows like *Sesame Street,* which teaches them that the world is full of friendly interracial adults and cute puppets and letters that form recognizable patterns. This is, of course, a pack of lies. When I was a kid, in New York, my friends and I watched shows like *Captain Video,* which taught us that the world was full of evil forces trying to destroy the earth, which turns out to be absolutely correct.

You remember SATs. You got your number-two pencils and sat in the cafeteria for two hours answering questions like this:

Fred wants to redo his bathroom in pink wallpaper, so he invites Sam over to help. If Fred's bathroom is eight feet by five feet and has a seven-foot ceiling, and each roll of wallpaper is thirty-two inches wide, how long will Sam take to realize there is something just a little bit strange about Fred?

Here is a tip on how to get good grades on your English papers: *Never say anything about a book that anybody with any common sense would say.* For example, suppose you are studying *Moby-Dick.* Anybody with any common sense would say Moby-Dick is a big white whale, since the characters in the book refer to it as a big white whale roughly eleven thousand times. So in *your* paper, *you* say Moby-Dick is actually the Republic of Ireland. Your professor, who is sick to death of reading papers and never liked *Moby-Dick* anyway, will think you are enormously creative. If you can regularly come up with lunatic interpretations of simple stories, you should major in English.

Babies do not take solid food through their mouths, which are generally occupied with other objects. Babies absorb solid food through their chins. You can save yourself a lot of frustrating effort if you smear the food directly on your baby's chin, rather than putting it in the baby's mouth and forcing the baby to expel it on to its chin, as so many uninformed parents do.

• • •

Babies *never* cry because their diapers are dirty. You change their diapers only to make *yourself* feel better. You could leave the same diaper on your baby for *months* and it would be perfectly happy, although considerably heavier and less pleasant to be around.

SAT tests are designed by huge panels of experts in education and psychology who work for *years* to design tests in which *not one single question measures any bit of knowledge that anyone might actually need in the real world.* We should *applaud* kids for getting lower scores.

You can either bottle-feed or breast-feed your baby. Many noted health fanatics strongly recommend that you breast-feed your baby on the grounds that it is very good for the baby. This may be true, but the *real* advantage of breast-feeding is that *only female persons can do it.* This means you male persons do not have to get up at the insane hours babies like to get up at.

Public Behavior Mode is a snotty behavior pattern that modern children get into because they know that modern parents aren't allowed to strike them in public for fear of being reported to the police as child abusers.

• • •

Extended Public Behavior Mode baffles medical science because in it a child can cry for more than forty-five minutes *without inhaling*.

Many kinds of baby food are available, all of them disgusting. Basically, the baby-food industry takes things that no normal human being would ever dream of eating, such as squash, and grinds them into mush and puts them in little jars. Babies, of course, hate baby food; they would much prefer the kinds of things *you* eat, such as cheeseburgers and beer. If we fed babies normal food, they would be full-grown, productive adults in a matter of weeks. But this would destroy the baby-food industry.

My son Rob, being twelve, is not legally required to obey the laws of gravity. Rob skis the way the Road Runner runs in cartoons. He looks for the steepest, scariest slope, one where the bottom is littered with the carcasses of mountain goats and professional rock climbers who died attempting to get down it. Without pausing, he launches himself off the edge, stops in midair to look around for several seconds, then *whoosh* turns into a blur and zips to the bottom, where he turns back—he is a tiny black dot now, way down the mountain—and shouts impatiently, "Come *on!* Beep Beep!"

If you don't have enough drama in your life, you need to chaperone a party for a group of seventh-graders. ("Chaperone" comes from the French words *chape,* meaning "person," and *rone,* meaning "who is aging very rapidly.")

• • •

I think we should have a program wherein our top scientific minds go into the public schools and lecture to the students, and if the students fool around, our top scientific minds should whack them on the head with slide rules.

My son told me that there are people called "posers" who *dress* like "bassers," but are in fact, secretly, "preppies." He said that some "posers" also pose as "headbangers," who are people who like heavy-metal music, which is performed by skinny men with huge hair who stomp around the stage, striking their instruments and shrieking angrily, apparently because someone has stolen all their shirts.

Remember how the news media made a big deal about it when those people came out after spending two years inside Biosphere 2? Well, two years is *nothing*. Veteran parents assure me that teenagers routinely spend that long in the *bathroom*.

Summer vacation is almost here. Soon it will be time for you parents to pile the kids into the car, show them how to work the ignition key, then watch them roar off down the street, possibly in reverse, as you head back into your house for two weeks of quiet relaxation.

If you want to put some "zing" back into your marriage, you should go to a "couples only" resort. This is a popular new type of resort that does not allow you to bring your children, the theory being that it is difficult for you and your spousal unit to get into a romantic mood if one of you has to pause every forty-five seconds to shout "JASON! I TOLD YOU NOT TO SQUIRT SUN BLOCK INTO ASHLEY'S EAR!"

During summer vacation, you are required by federal law to take your children to at least one historical or natural site featuring an educational exhibit with a little button that you're supposed to push, except that when you do, nothing happens, because all the little light bulbs, which were supposed to light up in an educational manner and tell The Story of Moss, burned out in 1973.

What matters is that you provide a memorable and rewarding and, above all, enjoyable vacation experience for your children whether they like it or not.

"DAMMIT, YOU KIDS," you might find yourself explaining to them, "IF YOU DON'T TAKE THOSE LEGOS OUT OF YOUR LITTLE BROTHER'S NOSE AND COME LOOK AT THIS EDUCATIONAL EXHIBIT THIS INSTANT, I SWEAR I WILL *NOT* TAKE YOU TO THE OYSTER KINGDOM THEME PARK."

I keep seeing young teenage males wearing enormous pants; pants that two or three teen-agers could occupy simultaneously and still have room in there for a picnic basket; pants that a clown would refuse to wear on the grounds that they were too undignified. The young men wear these pants really low, so that the waist is about knee level and the pants butt drags on the ground. . . . What I want to know is, how do young people buy these pants? Do they try them on to make sure they *don't* fit? Do they take along a 570-pound friend or a mature polar bear, and buy pants that fit *him?*

You should never set out on a family summer vacation without a complete set of parental threats. You cannot simply assume that when your children have, for example, locked somebody else's child inside the motel ice machine, you'll be able to come up with a good parental threat right there on the spot.

Contrary to what you hear from the "experts," it's a bad idea for parents and teenagers to attempt to communicate with each other, because there's always the risk that one of you will actually find out what the other one is thinking.

● ● ●

My son thinks it's a fine idea to stay up until 3 A.M. on school nights reading what are called "suspense novels," defined as "novels wherein the most positive thing that can happen to a character is that the Evil Ones will kill him *before* they eat his brain."

We recently had a party for our son's thirteenth birthday. We rented a Holiday Inn function room, on the theory that it was roomier and less flammable than our house. We hired two nice young DJs to play ugly music really loud so that the youngsters would enjoy it. We ordered a large quantity of cold cuts for the youngsters to ignore, as well as a nice fresh vegetable platter for them to actively avoid.

My son happens to be a boy, and he never went through the Barbie phase. He went through the Masters of the Universe phase. For two years our household was the scene of a fierce, unceasing battle between armies of good and evil action figures. They were everywhere. You'd open up the salad crisper, and there would be He-Man and Skeletor, striking each other with carrots.

By morning, my son and the bed have bonded into a single biological entity. Sometimes he has to go to school with his bed still attached to his body; this has really hurt his gym grade.

• • •

My son eats his breakfast in extreme slow motion with his eyes completely closed. He sometimes accidently puts food into his ear.

Now that my son has turned thirteen, I'm thinking about writing a self-help book for parents of teenagers. It would be a sensitive, insightful book that would explain the complex, emotionally charged relationship between the parent and the adolescent child. The title would be *I'm a Jerk; You're a Jerk.*

You never have to figure out what to get children, because they will tell you *exactly* what they want. They spend *months* researching these things on the Saturday-morning cartoon shows. Make sure you get exactly what they tell you to get, even if you disapprove of it. For example, if your child wants you to get Murderous Bob, the Doll with the Face You Can Rip Right Off, get it.

Today's modern, state-of-the-art little boy wants a robot that he can pretend is capable of, on Low Power, vaporizing Connecticut.

I bought this train set for my son on his first Christmas, when he was two months old and the only way he knew to play with it was by putting it in his mouth. So it developed some kind of serious train disorder, probably drool in the motor, and every year, when we finally get it hooked up and plugged in, it just sits there, humming. The Little Engine on Valium.

The Power Rangers are a group of low-IQ trailer-park dwellers who have extramarital affairs with their in-laws and screech at each other in front of a live studio audience. No, wait, that's the Jerry Springer show.

The Power Rangers are a group of teenagers who have the ability to transform themselves into crimefighters with the power to beat the living starch out of evil beings while speaking very bad dialogue.

Medical emergencies can occur on even the best-planned family trip. That's why, before you set out, you should familiarize yourself with the International Classification of Diseases (ICD), which is the system used to report medical problems to U.S. government agencies. Alert reader Denise Martin sent me a copy of the ICD, which classifies every conceivable kind of medical problem, including the following, which I am not making up:

E845—Accident in spacecraft
E912—Bean in nose
E966—Beheaded by guillotine
E906.8—Butted by animal
E842—Glider fire

E915—Hairball
E908—Injured by cloudburst
E912—Marble in nose
E906.8—Pecked by bird
E844—Sucked into jet aircraft

In 1965, we were not like you young males today, walking around in giant pants that are structurally identical to a Sears-brand four-person mountain tent with pockets. Back in 1965 we preferred extremely tight pants, the kind that you never put your hands in the pockets of, because you'd never get them back out. We did not wear those pants because of some trivial passing "fad"; We wore them because the Beatles wore them. We idolized the Beatles, except for those of us who idolized the Rolling Stones, who in those days still had many of their original teeth. We argued passionately about which band was better, Beatles vs. Stones, because we *cared about the issues.*

Social scientists released the surprising results of a nationwide sex survey showing that the average American married couple has sex 3.7 times per month, although they achieve mutual orgasmic climax only .2 times per month, because the other 3.5 times they are interrupted by a child pounding frantically on the door to announce, at 11:30 P.M., that he or she has a major school project due the following morning.

It's late October, and I'm watching my son play football.

Well, okay, he's not technically *playing*. He's on the sidelines, No. 85, standing near the coach, looking alert, hoping the coach will notice him and send him in. I'm not so sure this is a good idea, because the other team's players are extremely large. They're supposed to be junior-high students, but if they are, they apparently started junior high later in life, after having played a number of years for the Chicago Bears. They look *extremely* mature. You can actually see their beards growing. They probably have to shave in the huddle.

You could buy a wide variety of souvenirs at Superbowl XXIX. Do you want to know what priceless mementos my son, Rob, and his friend, Pablo, *both* chose to spend $25 apiece on, to serve as mementos of this once-in-a-lifetime athletic event? I will tell you: As souvenirs of Super Bowl XXIX, which as you may recall was a game between the San Francisco 49ers and the San Diego Chargers, Rob and Pablo purchased autographed photographs of O. J. Simpson. I swear I am not making this up. "Why?" I asked the boys. *"Why??"*

"They're gonna be worth a *lot* of money," they said. The Idealism of Youth.

Each year, the top toy-industry moguls hold a secret meeting where they decide what will be that year's hot toy (previous years' selections include the Cabbage Patch dolls and Barney the Really Irritating Dinosaur). The toy moguls then follow a two-pronged strategy:

Prong One: They stage a massive promotional campaign, thereby causing millions upon millions of young people ages three through eight to want this toy, and this toy alone, more than life itself.

Prong Two: They manufacture exactly four units of this toy.

The result is that you have rampaging mobs of parents, all desperately competing for the same unavailable toy, descending on Toys "R" Us stores and beating each other senseless with Tonka trucks. This is a sacred holiday retailing season tradition here in America, comparable to the tradition of putting up Santa Claus decorations at Halloween.

At my son's football game, the other team scores a touchdown, causing us Raider parents to groan. The Raider cheerleaders, however, remain undaunted. They have a cheer for just this situation. It goes (I am not making this cheer up): "They made a touchdown! But it's all right!" The Raider cheerleaders remain perky and upbeat no matter what happens in the game. This may be because they wisely refuse to look at the game. They face us parents, going through their routines, happy in their own totally separate cheerleading world. A plane could crash on the field and they might not notice, and even if they did, I bet it wouldn't seriously impact their perkiness ("A plane crashed on the field! But it's all right!")

My son, Rob, had no trouble at all snowboarding. None. In minutes he was cruising happily down the mountain; you could actually see his clothes getting baggier. I, on the other hand, spent most of my time lying on my back, groaning, while space-suited skiers swooped past and sprayed snow on me. If I hadn't gotten out of there, they'd have completely covered me; I now realize that the small hills you see on ski slopes are formed around the bodies of forty-seven-year-olds who tried to learn snowboarding.

If you're seeking a gift for a youngster in those hard-to-please teen years, then look no further, because he or she will definitely think that this gift concept is—in the lingo of today's "with-it" youngsters—"real groovy, man." These are trading cards, put out by the University of Michigan at Flint, featuring twenty-nine of the world's top economists. On one side of the cards are attractive black-and-white photographs of the economists, looking exactly like the kinds of studs and studettes that you would expect to find in top economist circles. On the other side of the cards is exciting information about the economist (". . . developed the methodology of input-output analysis"). We are certain that the teens on your list will spend many happy hours trading and discussing these cards.

My son and I can no longer ski together. We have a fundamental difference in technique: He skis via the Downhill Method, in which you ski down the hill; whereas I ski via the Breath-Catching Method, in which you stand sideways on the hill, looking as athletic as possible without actually moving muscles (this could cause you to start sliding down the hill). If anybody asks if you're okay, you say, "I'm just catching my breath!" in a tone of voice that suggests that at any moment you're going to swoop rapidly down the slope; whereas in fact you're planning to stay right where you are, rigid as a statue, until the spring thaw. At night, when the Downhillers have all gone home, we Breath-Catchers will still be up there, clinging to the mountainside, chewing on our parkas for sustenance.

My son is learning to drive. This terrifies me. He's four years old.

Well, technically he's fifteen. But from the perspective of the aging parent there is no difference between four and fifteen, except that when your child is four, his motoring privileges are restricted to little toy Fisher-Price people who are unlikely (although I would not totally rule it out, in America) to sue you.

My fifteen-year-old son, Rob, his fourteen-year-old friend Ryan, and I rented snowmobiles at a place called the Smiley Creek Lodge, which is in a place called Smiley Creek, which pretty much consists of the Smiley Creek Lodge. We also rented helmets and jumpsuits so that we would look as much as possible like the Invasion of the Dork Tourists from Space. A very nice man showed us how to make the snowmobiles go. He seemed extremely calm, considering that he was turning three powerful and expensive machines over to two adolescent boys and a humor columnist.

Anybody who bought into the Comet Hyakutake hype had to be a total moron. Like me, for example. I can't explain it. One minute I was reading the comet story in the *Miami Herald*, and the next minute, like Charlie Brown getting suckered into trying to kick the football yet another time, I was saying to my son: "Rob, let's go see the comet!" He said okay, probably because he's fifteen—an age at which you find your parents hideously embarrassing—and he figured that if we went to a dark, remote area, there was less chance that his friends would see him with me.

In Florida, when your child turns fifteen, the state lets him obtain a permit that allows him to drive an actual car on actual roads, despite the fact that you can vividly remember when he slept on Return of the Jedi sheets. Of course there are restrictions: He must be accompanied by a licensed driver age eighteen or over. But that does not reassure me. What that means to me is that, in the eyes of the state of Florida, it is perfectly okay for my son to be driving around accompanied only by Ted Kennedy.

A while ago the *New York Times* printed an item concerning an eleven-year-old girl who was overheard on the streets of East Hampton, New York, telling her father, "Daddy, Daddy, please don't sing!"

The daddy was Billy Joel.

The irony, of course, is that a lot of people would pay *big* money to hear Billy Joel sing. But of course these people are not Billy Joel's adolescent offspring. To his adolescent offspring, Billy Joel represents the same thing that all parents represent to their adolescent offspring: Bozo-Rama. To an adolescent, there is nothing in the world more embarrassing than a parent.

I want the law to say that if my son is going to drive, he must be accompanied by a licensed paramedic and at least two Supreme Court justices. Also, I believe that, as a safety precaution, his car should be attached via a stout chain to a restraining device such as the Pentagon.

It's not that I think my son is a bad driver. He's actually a pretty good driver, careful to signal his turns. That's what worries me: He'll be driving in Miami, where nobody, including the police, does this. If Miami motorists were to see a turn signal, they could become alarmed and start shooting.

The original cause of brain sludge is your parents. After you were born, your parents decided to put something into your brain, but instead of information you'd need—for example, the PIN number to your ATM card—they sang drivel to you, the same drivel that parents have been dumping into children's brains since the Middle Ages, such as "Pop Goes the Weasel." Your parents were in fact starting the sludge-buildup process, not realizing every word they put into your brain would stay there *forever*, so that decades later you'd wake up in the middle of the night wondering: *Why? WHY did she cut off their tails with a carving knife?*

When I was an adolescent, my dad wore one of those Russian-style hats that were semipopular with middle-aged guys for a while in the early '60s. You may remember this hat: It was shaped kind of like those paper hats that some fast-food workers have to wear, only it was covered with fur. Nobody—and I include both Mel Gibson and the late Cary Grant in this statement—could wear this hat and not look like a dork.

So naturally my dad wore one.

Today's young people are much more interested in basketball, football, soccer, and downloading dirty pictures from the Internet. But in my youth, baseball ruled. Almost all of us boys played in Little League, a character-building experience that helped me develop a personal relationship with God.

"God," I would say, when I was standing in deep right field—the coach put me in right field only because it was against the rules to put me in Sweden, where I would have done less damage to the team—"please please *please* don't let the ball come to me."

Yes, parents: In the ongoing battle between you and your adolescent children, you possess the ultimate weapon—the Power to Embarrass. Use this power, parents! If your adolescent children are in *any* way displeasing you—if they are mouthing off or engaging in unacceptable behavior—do not waste your breath nagging them. Instead, simply sing. In fact, I think our judicial system should use this power to punish teenage criminal defendants.

Judge: Young man, this is your third offense. I'm afraid I'm going to have to give you the maximum sentence.

Youthful Defendant: No! Not . . .

Judge: Yes. I'm going to ask your mom to get up here on the court karaoke machine and sing *Copacabana.*

Youthful Defendant: NO! SEND ME TO JAIL!

Eventually my father stopped being a hideous embarrassment to me, and I, grasping the Torch of Dorkhood, became a hideous embarrassment to my son, especially when I try to sing like Aretha Franklin. If you want to see a flagrant and spectacular violation of the known laws of physics, watch what my son does if we are in a public place and for some reason I need to burst into the opening lines of "Respect" *(WHAT you want! Baby I got it!).* When this happens, my son's body will instantaneously disappear into another dimension and rematerialize as far as two football fields away. The results are even more dramatic with the song *"Got My Mojo Workin'."*

My son, Rob, and his friend Ryan are wonderful and intelligent boys, but they have the common sense of table salt, which they demonstrated when we went snowmobiling in Idaho. It's not their fault: Their brains have not yet developed the Fear Lobe. If you give them control over a motorized vehicle, they are going to go at the fastest possible speed, which on a modern snow-mobile turns out to be 14,000 miles per hour. They were leaving trails of flaming snow behind them. I tried to exercise Adult Supervision by yelling "HEY! GUYS! BE CAREFUL! HEY!" but they couldn't hear me, because sound travels only so fast.

Scientists calculate that the attraction between a child and his or her bed on a school morning can be up to seventy-five times as strong as mere gravity. Most parents try to overcome this attraction by pounding on the door and shouting ineffective threats, the most popular one being "YOU'RE GOING TO BE LATE FOR SCHOOL!" The problem with this threat is that it's based on the idiotic premise that the child wants to be in school and be forced to sit on a hard chair and figure out how many times seven goes into fifty-six; naturally, the child prefers the bed.

My son is a senior in high school, which means I've gone on several college visits and attended several college orientation sessions. As part of these sessions, the kids have interviews with college officials. My son revealed little about what goes on in these interviews, but my theory is that the officials close the door and say: "Relax. You'll spend the majority of college attending parties, playing Hacky Sack, and watching *Friends*. The tour is purely for the parents. The guides make up the building names as they go along."

Out West, we encountered numerous families that, after many hours together in the minivan, had reached Critical Hostility Mass. We saw a family stopped at a roadside area overlooking a mountain vista, but nobody was looking at it. Two boys were slumped in the backseat with their baseball caps jammed over their eyes, listening to individual compact disc players. A girl, maybe twelve, was stomping tearfully away from the van, followed by Mom, waving bread and shouting, "IF YOU DON'T EAT THIS SANDWICH, I'M NOT MAKING YOU ANOTHER ONE!" A few feet away, Dad was sitting on a rock, chewing slowly, staring at the ground. Togetherness!

I love Halloween. It reminds me of my childhood days as a student at Wampus Elementary School in Armonk, New York, when we youngsters used to celebrate Halloween by making decorations out of construction paper and that white paste that you could eat. This is also how we celebrated Columbus Day, Washington's Birthday, Lincoln's Birthday, Thanksgiving, Christmas, Easter, New Year's, Valentine's Day, Mother's Day, Father's Day, Armistice Day, Flag Day, Arbor Day, Thursday, etc. We brought these decorations home to our parents, who by federal law were required to attach them to the refrigerator with magnets.

believe that we parents must encourage our children to become educated, so they can get into a good college that we cannot afford.

I try to help my son, Rob, with his schooling, but over the years this has become more difficult. Back when he was dealing with basic educational issues such as why the sky is blue and what a duck says, I always knew the correct answers ("It doesn't matter" and "Moo"). But when Rob got into the higher grades, he started dealing with complex concepts such as the "hypotenuse," which hadn't been invented yet when I was a student.

Women have low self-esteem regarding their appearance. Why? Barbie. Girls grow up playing with a doll proportioned such that, if it were a human, it would be seven feet tall and weigh eighty-one pounds, of which fifty-three pounds would be bosoms. Contrast that standard with the standard set for little boys by their dolls . . . excuse me, by their action figures. Most of the action figures that my son played with when he was little were hideous looking. For example, he was very fond of an action figure called "Buzz-Off," who was part human, part flying insect. Buzz-Off was not a looker. But he was extremely self-confident. You could not imagine Buzz-Off saying to the other action figures, "Do you think these wings make my hips look big?"

So your school is having a science fair! Great! The science fair has long been a favorite educational tool in the American school system, and for a good reason: Your teachers hate you.

Ha ha! No, seriously, although a science fair can seem like a big "pain," it can help you understand important scientific principles, such a Newton's First Law of Inertia, which states, "A body at rest will remain at rest until 8:45 P.M. the night before the science-fair project is due, at which point the body will come rushing to the body's parents, who are already in their pajamas, and shout, *'I just remembered the science fair is tomorrow and we gotta go to the store right now!'"*

My son is a senior in high school, which means that pretty soon he'll probably select a college. We've already gone on several college visits. Most college visits include an orientation session, wherein you sit in a lecture room and a college official tells you impressive statistics about the college, including, almost always, how small the classes are. Class smallness is considered the ultimate measure of how good a college is. Harvard, for example, has zero students per class: The professors just sit alone in their classrooms, filing their nails.

Once you have returned home on the night before your science fair project is due and folded your Official Science Fair Display Board into three sections (allow six hours) it's time to start thinking about what kind of project to do. Prize-winning projects clearly demonstrate an interesting scientific principle. So forget about winning a prize. What you need is a project that can be done at 1 A.M. using materials found in your house. Ideally, it should also involve a minimum of property damage or death, which is why, on the advice of legal counsel, we are not going to discuss some popular project topics such as "What Is Inside Plumbing?" and "Flame-Proofing Your Cat."

During the summer, Dad should be in charge of the cooking, because only Dad, being a male of the masculine gender, has the mechanical "know-how" to operate a piece of technology as complex as a barbecue grill. To be truly traditional, the grill should be constructed of the following materials:

- 4 percent "rust-resistant" steel;

- 58 percent rust;

- 23 percent hardened black grill scunge from food cooked as far back as 1987 (the scunge should never be scraped off, because it is what is actually holding the grill together);

- 15 percent spiders.

One evening my wife mentioned she had been talking to the son of one of her friends, a boy named Alexander, about his fourth birthday. "Alexander says he's having a Batman party," my wife said.

"Hm," I said.

"I told him maybe Batman would come to the party," my wife said.

"Hm," I said.

My wife said nothing then. She just looked at me.

Suddenly, I knew I was going to be Batman.

I was not opposed. It seemed to me Batman had a pretty neat life, disguised as playboy Bruce Wayne, waiting for the police commissioner to shine the Bat Signal onto the clouds (it was always a cloudy night when the commissioner needed Batman). Then Bruce would change into his costume and roar off in the Batmobile to do battle with the Forces of Evil or attend a birthday party.

My son, like millions of other high school seniors, will have to make a crucial decision, the consequences of which will remain with him for the rest of his life: Who will be his prom date?

Also, at some point he'll probably select a college. In fact, we've already gone on several college visits, which are helpful in choosing a college because you can get answers to important academic questions such as:

- Is there parking?

- Are all the students required to get body piercings? Or is this optional at the undergraduate level?

- Is there a bank near the college that you can rob to pay the tuition?

It goes without saying that you cannot send your child back to school without a compass and a protractor. A compass is a thing with a sharp point and a little mutant pencil that is always falling out. A protractor is a thing that you always get when you get a compass. It is a centuries-old tradition for children to go back to school with these devices, even though nobody has the faintest idea what their educational purpose is, other than using the metal point to carve bad words into desks. A spokesperson for the American Compass and Protractor Manufacturers Association told us, "We sell twenty-three million of these things every September, and we lie awake at night asking ourselves, *why?*"

A traditional item you should have on your child's back-to-school list is some kind of notebook. I know there are many kinds of new-fangled "high-tech" notebooks on the market today, but for my money, the old-fashioned three-ring binder that I used as a schoolboy remains, as an educational tool, one of the most useless things ever invented. I spent basically all of my classroom time from 1955 through 1963 trying to repair torn notebook paper with those stupid "reinforcing rings" that were always gumming themselves together into a little defensive clot. It cannot be without coincidence that during these same years, the Soviet Union surged way ahead in the Space Race.

If you want to get a good grade on a science fair project, you have to do a project that will impress your teachers. Here's a proven winner:

"Hypothesis—That (Name of Teacher) and (Name of Another Teacher) would prefer that I not distribute the photo I took of them when they were 'chaperoning' our class trip to Epcot Center and they ducked behind the cottage-cheese exhibit in the Amazing World of Curds."

Depending on your research, you might get more than a good grade from your teachers: You might get money! Science truly can be rewarding.

My son was assigned the epic poem *Beowulf*. I have never been a fan of *Beowulf,* or epic poems in general. "Epic," in my opinion, is a code word English teachers use for "boring," the same way they use "satirical" to mean "you will not laugh once." Nevertheless I stressed to Rob that he should make this assignment a priority, allowing nothing to come ahead of it, but that first we would go out for Italian food. I like to do this with Rob because he always orders pizza, which I am not allowed to eat because it contains cholesterol, but it is a scientific fact that your body will not absorb cholesterol if you take it from another person's plate.

I've gone on several college visits with my son. In college orientation sessions, many kids seem semibored, whereas parents not only take notes, but also ask questions, sometimes indicating that they've mapped out their children's academic careers through death. There will be some girl who looks like she's eleven years old, and her dad will raise his hand and say, "If my daughter declares a quadruple major in Biology, Chemistry, Physics, and Large Scary Equations, and she graduates with honors and then earns doctorates in Medicine, Engineering, Law, Architecture, Dentistry, and Taxidermy, and then she qualifies for a Merwanger Fellowship for Interminable Postdoctoral Studies, does the Nobel organization pay her expenses to Sweden to pick up her prize?"

These days, I'm useless to my son, Rob, as an educational resource, except on those rare occasions when he is studying a topic I'm familiar with. For example, last year, in history class, he studied the '60s. That's right: The '60s are now considered a historical period, just like the Roman Empire, except that as far as modern kids are concerned, the '60s featured stupider haircuts. Because I lived through that era, when Rob asked me about it, I was able to give him helpful information.

"What did you do during the '60s?" he asked.

"None of your business," I informed him.

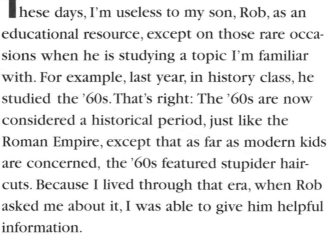

I like to let my son, Rob, drive because it improves my circulation by causing my heart to beat 175,000 times per minute. Although one trip we made was fairly relaxing, right up until Rob made the rookie error of actually stopping at a red light rather than accelerating through it as is customary in Miami, the result being that we were rammed by the car behind us.

It took two hours and two police officers to sort it out, with the outcome being that the other driver received a ticket. My car sustained only superficial damage, which I'm sure at today's body-work prices can be repaired for no more than it would cost to purchase the entire contents of the Louvre at retail.

My son is a senior in high school, which means I've attended several college orientation sessions. I have not given that much thought to my son's academic goals. I assumed he was going to college for the reason I did, which is that at some point they stop letting you go to high school. I tried to think of questions to ask the college officials, but the only one I could think of was, "How come these lecture hall desks are never designed for us left-handed people?" Although I didn't ask this, because it's probably insensitive on college campuses to say "left-handed people." You probably have to say something like "persons of left-handedness."

The college visit always includes a campus tour conducted by a student who is required to tell you the name of every single building on the campus, no matter how many there are ("Over there is the Gwendolyn A. Heckenswacker Institute for the Study of Certain Asian Mollusks, which we call 'the Heck.' And over there is the Myron and Gladys B. Prunepocket Center for Musty Old Books that Nobody Ever Looks At. And right next to that is The Building Right Next to the Myron and Gladys . . . ").

My teenage son's goal in life is to make me feel 3,500 years old. We'll be in the car and he'll say, "You wanna hear my new CD?" And I, flattered that he thinks his old man might like his music, will say "Sure!" So he increases the volume from "4" to "Meteor impact," and puts in a CD by a band with a name like "Pustule," and the next thing I know nuclear bass notes have activated the air bags, and I'm writhing, screaming for mercy with blood spurting three feet from my ears. My son then ejects the CD, smiling contentedly, knowing he has purchased a winner. On those rare occasions when I like one of his CDs, I imagine he destroys it with a blowtorch.